Original title:
Venusian Verses

Copyright © 2025 Creative Arts Management OÜ
All rights reserved.

Author: Ethan Prescott
ISBN HARDBACK: 978-1-80567-845-8
ISBN PAPERBACK: 978-1-80567-966-0

Love's Light in Stellar Shadows

In the glow of a neon star,
Two lovers dance from near to far.
They stumble on cosmic dust,
A leap of love, a little trust.

With comets crashing, oh what a sight,
They giggle in the galactic night.
A twist of fate, they trip and fall,
Floating in space, they laugh through it all.

A Martian chef with wormy stew,
Served strange delights, just for two.
Grinning wide with every bite,
Who knew odd flavors felt so right!

As asteroids race on a wild spree,
They twirl and glide with glee, oh me!
In their playful, starry embrace,
Love lights up the cosmic space.

Chasing the Eternal Dawn

In the morning light, we prance,
Chasing shadows in a dance,
With pancakes flipping in the breeze,
And giggles echoing through the trees.

The sun peeks out, a cheeky grin,
Winking down, let the games begin,
We spin like tops in a warm embrace,
Laughter bubbling up, a silly race.

Mysteries Beneath the Veil

Behind the curtain, secrets hide,
A cat in a hat takes us for a ride,
With wisdom from a wise old frog,
Who croaks out riddles through the fog.

What's that buzzing? What's that clatter?
An alien sipping on space-fresh batter,
He winks and nods, wearing a crown,
In a world where socks are always brown.

Gilded Horizons

Out on a boat made of gold,
We sail to shores of stories untold,
With fish that sing and waves that laugh,
We splash and twirl on a silly half.

The sunsets shimmer in shades of jam,
As jellybeans rain down like a spam,
We toast with cups of fizzy soda,
And dance like no one's asked our quota.

The Allure of Shining Realms

In a realm where unicorns cheat,
And dragons serve us cotton candy sweet,
We ride on clouds made of meringue,
With choruses sung by a marshmallow gang.

The stars above play hide and seek,
While comets do a little tweak,
We laugh till our bellies start to ache,
In this land where dreams are always fake.

Secrets of a Shimmering Sky

Stars wink with joy, wearing shades at night,
While comets throw parties, oh what a sight!
Aliens dance silly, in their bright space suits,
Flapping their arms, in their light-up boots.

Galaxies giggle, as planets play hide,
With rings made of jellybeans swirling wide.
Suns don sunglasses, basking in the glow,
While moons do the cha-cha, putting on a show.

Dance of the Planetary Veils

Planets prance proudly, as music starts to swell,
With each twirl and whirl, they cast a spell.
Asteroids join in, with a clumsy cheer,
Bumping and grinding, oh bring out the beer!

Venus spins with laughter, her veil in a twist,
Mercury races hard, it can't be dismissed.
Jupiter hops high, wanting to impress,
While Saturn just giggles, covered in confetti dress.

Poetry from the Cosmic Heart

Words float like bubbles, in the cosmic breeze,
Tickling the stars, with such vibrant ease.
Each verse a rocket, blasting off in rhyme,
Sailing through nebulae, lost in time.

Galactic gnomes scribble, on comets made of cheese,
Their thoughts tickle black holes, bringing them to knees.

Poetry shines bright, like a supernova spark,
Lighting up the universe, sending joy in the dark.

Petals of an Alien Bloom

Flowers on Mars wear hats and fake mustaches,
Playing cards with craters, making divas of ashes.
Each petal a pun, each stem a cute quirk,
Bees buzzing jokes, as they do their work.

Roses on Pluto rave, spinning like tops,
While daisies on Mercury pull off funny flops.
Alien blooms giggle, with deep cosmic cheer,
Sending out petals, planting smiles year by year.

The Touch of Celestial Breath

In a realm where laughter sings,
Alien fish wear tiny rings.
Gravity's a playful prank,
While space squirrels ride the tank.

Jupiter's got the best hairdo,
With moonbeams hiding in his shoe.
Stars twinkle at the cosmic joke,
As comets spin and giggle, poke.

Whispers from the Cosmic Sea

Galaxies swim with starry glee,
Mermaids laugh in zero-degree.
Waves of stardust tickle the ear,
As planets joke, 'It's much too clear!'

Neptune's dancing on a cloud,
With Saturn's rings as a stage, loud.
They sing of snacks from asteroids,
And cosmic pies that can't be avoided.

Eyes Reflecting the Stars

Eyes twinkle like the night-time sky,
With tiny winks that say, oh my!
Each glance bursts like a shooting star,
Making wishes that travel far.

With a look, the moon starts to hum,
And Martian bugs begin to drum.
The universe is a playful tale,
With every blink, we dance and sail.

Poetic Constellations

Constellations giggle in lines,
While shooting stars swear like fine wines.
Ursa Major can't stop to chat,
As Little Dip lifts a giant hat.

Orion trips on his own belt,
As cosmic cheese gives him a melt.
The Milky Way spills jokes from above,
Mistakes made by the stars we love.

Celestial Connections

In the sky, I lost my shoe,
Thought it was a star, it's true!
Then a comet winked and swayed,
Guess it's just a cosmic parade.

Aliens called, they want to chat,
Said they found my missing hat!
We laughed and danced through the night,
In their spaceship, what a sight!

Embracing the Horizon

A silhouette on Mars, I see,
Is that a friend or just a tree?
With arms wide, I take a leap,
And land on something soft, not deep.

Turns out it's a giant pie,
Shooting stars fly as I sigh,
A slice on Saturn, how divine!
Next stop, Pluto, for some wine!

Mysteries of a Distant Glow

What's that twinkle? A big grin?
Oh wait, it's just my pet hamster's chin!
He's stargazing from my bed,
While dreaming of cosmic bread.

He claims he's from another place,
With rocket ships and lots of space.
I nod along - what a champ,
When he curls up, all snug and damp!

Poems of the Evening Star

The evening star is quite the tease,
With its sparkles and subtle breeze.
It laughs as it flirts with the moon,
Who replies with a hum and a tune.

They argue of who shines the best,
While I munch on popcorn, all pressed.
The sky giggles, in bright delight,
With heavenly mischief on this night.

The Luminous Pursuit

In a world where sparkles dance,
A penguin tried to woo a prance.
He wore a tie, quite out of place,
While chasing stars in outer space.

With a wink and a dance so bright,
He stumbled through the moonlit night.
Each comet tail a chance to sway,
But his best moves went all astray.

He offered cheese, what a delight!
To alien friends with eyes so bright.
A lunar fox said, 'What a score!'
As they all rolled on the cosmic floor.

The pursuit was wild, a chummy chase,
In a universe, full of quirky grace.
With laughter loud among the stars,
They spun and twirled near Jupiter's bars.

Spheres of Desire

In circles round, they twirled like sprites,
A toaster fell for a kitchen light.
'Toaster, dear, you're just too hot!'
They giggled in their quirky plot.

A blender joined, it blended well,
With hopes to mix and make love swell.
But burnt toast cried, 'I'm just too brown!'
While all the others spun around.

Made of steel but hearts so warm,
They dreamed of love beyond the norm.
In a cosmic kitchen, wild and grand,
They stirred a soup with humor at hand.

So next time you seek cosmic spice,
Remember the laughter, that's the nice.
For in the spheres of clumsy delight,
Love's kitchen rocks through day and night.

Threads of the Divine Light

Cosmic kittens stitched the skies,
With yarns of stars and silly sighs.
They knitted dreams with fuzzy paws,
Creating laughter 'neath heavenly laws.

Patterns of jokes, like comets, flew,
With rainbows bright in every hue.
One stitch said, 'Life's a wild kite!'
Another laughed, 'Let's take flight!'

A grandma star brought cookies sweet,
While black holes danced to the beat.
With cosmic crumbs, they spread good cheer,
Each thread a giggle, warm and clear.

So as you weave your daily plight,
Remember those threads of pure delight.
For in the cosmos, bright and bold,
Laughter's the fabric, tales unfold.

Orbital Love Letters

A martian wrote from far away,
In craters deep, he found his way.
With charming words, he sent a shout,
'To extraterrestrials, no doubt!'

His rocket pen was full of flair,
As he scribbled love in fragrant air.
He sent a note with glitter dust,
Promising warmth, a cosmic trust.

The moon replied with a glowing beam,
'While I'm silver, you're such a dream!'
An asteroid joined with jokes galore,
'Our love's not rocky, it's never a bore!'

So if you wonder how love persists,
Look to the cosmos, and giggle at twists.
For in orbital letters, far and wide,
Laughter's the rocket, love as the guide.

A Love Born Among the Stars

In a rocket ship made of cheese,
Two hearts floated with such ease.
They danced among the cosmic dust,
Laughing loudly, oh they must!

A comet winked, they caught its eye,
Promised love that would not die.
Cosmic giggles filled the air,
Who knew space could be a fair?

With alien flowers in their hair,
They took selfies without a care.
Starry skies held their sweet dreams,
Making wishes with moonbeam gleams.

In zero gravity, love did spin,
Around their hearts, a playful din.
Galactic popcorn in their hands,
Together they made amazing plans.

Celestial Reveries

On a planet made of silly hats,
They shared jokes with the fuzzy cats.
Sipping stardust from a cup,
Their laughter echoed, all went up.

Meteors danced to their own beat,
As they waltzed on comet's heat.
Snorting giggles, in delight,
Each wish a spark, so pure, so bright.

Jupiter chuckled at their glee,
While Saturn wiggled, can't you see?
They spun 'round rings of ice and light,
Creating joy through cosmic flight.

With dreams that soared beyond the stars,
They found love in the strange avatars.
As echoes of laughter filled the night,
They painted the cosmos with pure delight.

Ephemeral Whispers of Infinity

In a black hole, they lost their socks,
But found each other, like two clocks.
Ticking time in a merry chase,
Fueled by love and a little space.

From stardust soup, they brewed their stew,
Adding laughter as the secret glue.
A sprinkle of quarks, a dash of fun,
Underneath a billion suns.

With each whisper of the vast unknown,
They built a castle from what was grown.
A world where giggles never cease,
Embracing doubts with light and peace.

As they bounced from star to big black void,
Every moment felt joyfully deployed.
In the echoes of infinity, so wild,
Two silly lovers, forever a child.

The Glow of Timeless Love

Underneath a sky of candyfloss,
Their hearts would dance, they were the boss.
With moonlit serenades, they'd sway,
In their own cosmic ballet.

A nebula wrapped them close in glee,
While stars sparkle, so carefree.
Meteor showers, a nightly show,
Their love was a supernova glow.

Crisp cosmic pies they would bake,
Sharing slices as they'd quake.
Every giggle, a twinkling spark,
Shining bright, lighting the dark.

Through comets that zoomed and crossed,
In laughter, they found what never was lost.
In a universe wide and so absurd,
They sipped joy from every word.

Memories From a Glimmering Realm

In a realm where giggles bloom,
Dancing lights chase away the gloom.
Silly stars with wiggly beams,
Making wishes, crafting dreams.

Bouncing planets in a race,
Tripping over glitter's grace.
Jelly comets plop and splat,
Alien cows say, "Look at that!"

Saucers swirl with pastel treats,
Martian music in catchy beats.
Gummy worms on fluffy pies,
Space-time tickles, oh what a surprise!

Under moons of candy cheer,
Laughter echoes far and near.
In this world of jolly fun,
Every day is a wild run!

Chasing Shadows in Starlight

Chasing shadows, quite absurd,
Twinkling winks from a chirpy bird.
Moonbeams peek around the corner,
While we dance like quirky mourner.

Space whales sing with goofy glee,
Flipping pancakes, just for me!
Shooting stars in a wink costume,
Racing past the cosmic loom.

Nebulae wear splattered paint,
Making giants laugh, it ain't quaint.
A comet stalls, has to sneeze,
Showering us with cosmic cheese.

In the dark, we laugh and hide,
Snickering where shadows abide.
With every twinkle, cheeky sprites,
Pull our legs in wild delights!

The Allure of an Otherworldly Embrace

An embrace from beyond the sky,
With aliens who love to fry.
A hug transforms into confetti,
As we laugh, our shirts get heavy.

Tentacles tickle; what a surprise,
Eyes pop wide, like playful pies.
Feeling giddy in the swirl,
As rocket sauce begins to whirl.

Grobots giggle, join the game,
As we shout each other's name.
In this wacky space-time dance,
We tumble, giggle—when's our chance?

With laughter ringing through the stars,
We barter glee for candy bars.
An allure that pulls us near,
In cosmic fun, we persevere!

A Celestial Tapestry

A tapestry hung high in space,
Woven threads of a smiling face.
Suns aflame in wild array,
Dancing colors light our play.

Quirky stitches, cosmic fibers,
Wiggly moons, the universe wipers.
Every thread a story tells,
Where humor by the starlight swells.

Planets wear polka-dotted gowns,
Giggles echo, music frowns.
Asteroids roll like laughter's spark,
As we frolic in the dark.

In this fabric of pure delight,
We bounce from day into the night.
A heavenly quilt, laughter's embrace,
Knit with joy, a smiling space!

Celestial Ink and Cosmic Pages

In a galaxy far, jokes take flight,
Planets giggle, stars laugh all night.
Comets dance with a splash of gin,
Writing silly tales on a whim.

Asteroids don hats, and they dine,
On cosmic snacks, it's quite divine.
Black holes chuckle, they're quite the jest,
Spinning tales of humor, they're the best.

Nebulae paint with coffee stains,
Crafting puns that tickle our brains.
Quasars wink with a twinkling eye,
As shooting stars zoom by and sigh.

In this vast expanse of playful art,
Galactic giggles bring joy to the heart.
With every turn of the cosmic page,
Laughter resonates, like a timeless rage.

The Heartbeat of Distant Worlds

Mars is dancing, oh what a sight,
With tiny robots, they groove all night.
Saturn's rings are a hula hoop,
While Jupiter's storms have the best of group.

Pluto's just chilling, small but bold,
Serving ice cream that's sprinkled with gold.
Mercury rushes, always in a race,
While Venus struts with a glamorous grace.

Satellite orbits, a spinning tease,
Sending signals, "Please come and seize!"
Uranus spins, a little askew,
While Neptune's laughing, "You too, you too!"

In this cosmic rhythm, worlds collide,
With every heartbeat, side by side.
Galactic giggles echo afar,
What a funny, whimsical bizarre!

Ethereal Love in the Cosmos

Two stars meet in a sparkling night,
Whispering softly, "You're my delight!"
They twinkle and wink, in cosmic cheer,
Sending love letters to each other near.

The moon blushes, a smile so wide,
As asteroids giggle in the night tide.
Galaxies swirl in a joyous spree,
Creating a dance between you and me.

With space dust sprinkled, they flirt and tease,
Sending comets on romantic keys.
Light-years apart, yet hearts are tight,
In this vast cosmos, love takes flight.

And while planets rotate, laughs are shared,
In the universe's book, love's declared.
Ethereal beings with laughter gold,
Spinning tales of love, forever bold.

Echoes of a Starlit Desire

In the dark, stardust dreams ignite,
With echoes of laughter, oh what a sight!
Meteor showers shower puns with grace,
As black holes chuckle in this endless space.

The sun winks brightly, a golden tease,
While planets orbit in effortless ease.
"Hey, did you hear? The moon's on a date,"
Said Mars with a grin, "It's going great!"

Galactic whispers float through the night,
As comets zoom past with dazzling light.
In this realm of wonder, joy will blare,
For starlit desires, are beyond compare.

So raise a toast to the cosmos wild,
Where love and laughter dance like a child.
In the echo of stars, desires expand,
New jokes are written in shimmering sand.

A Dance of Mercurial Lights

In the sky, where oddballs play,
Juggling stars in a quirky way,
Planets twirl with zest and zeal,
A cosmic show, a galactic reel.

Comets crash, they laugh and spin,
With Saturn's rings—what a din!
Neptune dips, his breezy flare,
While Jupiter's moons start dancing there.

Slipping past in meteor style,
Winking lights that tease and beguile,
A lunar pirouette unfolds,
In a dance of dreams, adventure bold!

Oh, the laughter among the spheres,
Echoes bright, erasing fears,
As each celestial buddy jives,
In this show, joyfully alive!

Planetary Dreams

In swirling forms, a merry crew,
With Martian pranks of red and blue,
Earth giggles, spinning round her friends,
In laughter, the universe extends.

Pluto peeks from his chilly shade,
With icy jokes, delightful charade,
While Venus teases with her charm,
Playing tricks, no cause for alarm!

Mercury zips with lightning glee,
His speed a comical sight to see,
While Saturn laughs, his rings take flight,
A carnival of color, pure delight!

Through cosmic realms, the dreams take shape,
Each planet crafting a funnyscape,
In a whirl of joy, they all convene,
A celestial party, a whimsical scene!

Flames of the Horizon

The sun throws jests in golden rays,
As laughter mingles in fiery plays,
With fiery clowns that dance and leap,
Spinning yarns that shimmer and sweep.

A comet crashes—a flaming kite,
Chasing shadows, a comical sight,
While the stars throw beans at the moon's face,
In this planetary jokeful race.

Planets bounce like balls on strings,
Jovial tunes that each one sings,
In the horizon, where dreams ignite,
Whimsical flames dance through the night!

Galaxies play peek-a-boo in style,
With cosmic giggles that stretch a mile,
In the fervent glow of twilight's cheer,
Every flame whispers, "Come join us here!"

Secrets of the Shimmering Sphere

Behind each twinkle, secrets hide,
With giggles shared, oh what a ride!
A wink from Mars, a silly grin,
Inviting all to join the spin!

Stars wear hats in wobbly ways,
Casting shadows for cosmic plays,
While planets puzzle in a trance,
Waltzing close, it's a funny dance!

Each shooting star is a jester bright,
Whirling tales in the depths of night,
Saturn's rings giggle and mock,
While cosmic critters play the clock.

A celestial circus up in the skies,
With laughter that never, ever dies,
In the shimmering sphere, secrets soar,
Fun erupts—who could ask for more?

A Chorus of Cosmic Hearts

In a galaxy where giggles grow,
Planets spin with a silly show.
Stars wink at quirks, all aglow,
Jovial dreams in cosmic tow.

Aliens play hopscotch on Mars,
While laughing comets race from afar.
Galactic jesters jump in cars,
Making wishes on candy bars.

Space whales sing in oddest tunes,
Juggling planets with oversized spoons.
Dancing through our funny balloons,
Chasing moonbeams and silly raccoons.

In laughter's grip, we'll drift and dart,
Unrehearsed lines from a shared heart.
Cosmic comedy, the best part,
In this universe, we'll never part.

Secrets of the Radiant Sphere

Beneath the glow of a tangerine sun,
Secret whispers of laughter begun.
Silly secrets, they wheel and run,
In the palace of joy, we're all one.

The clouds wear hats, oh what a sight,
Bouncing breezes dance in delight.
With giggles shared under starlit night,
The universe chuckles, so bright.

Asteroids dressed for a fancy ball,
Twirl like dancers, making us all fall.
In cosmic chaos, we hear the call,
Laughter's the magic that binds us all.

With each chuckle, the cosmos spins,
Opening hearts as the laughter begins.
In every wink, the joy always wins,
Glimmers of happiness, our beloved sins.

The Dance of Light and Love

Stars in tutus do the cha-cha,
While asteroids laugh, 'Oh la-la!'
Moonbeams shower in a twinkling spa,
Cosmic laughter brightens the euphoria.

Galaxies twirl in a disco haze,
While comets groove in moonlit bays.
Each flare of light, a silly phase,
Dancing through the vibrant maze.

Nebulas flicker, painting the night,
Bubbly aliens throw a light fight.
In the cosmic party, all feels right,
Here, every moment is pure delight.

With each step, we drift and sway,
In the cosmos where jokes play.
Laughter echoes, come what may,
Join the dance; it's a cosmic ballet.

Celestial Harmonics

In a symphony of stars that sing,
Neutron notes on a bouncy spring.
Playful planets do their thing,
    Galactic giggles in the ring.

Shooting stars play tag with time,
Harmonies sprout like silly rhyme.
Venus plays the kazoo in prime,
Creating tunes that feel sublime.

Wormholes whirl, a merry-go-round,
While sunbeams boogie to that funky sound.
In the warm embrace of joy profound,
Laughter in space, forever unbound.

As celestial bodies sway and twirl,
A cosmic chorus begins to unfurl.
In playful waves, our hearts will whirl,
The universe spins in a joyous swirl.

Harmonies of Celestial Passion

In a realm where lovebirds glide,
Planetary pizzas on the side.
Starlight sprinkled on our cake,
Gravity's pull, for love's own sake.

Dancing moons in pairs they twirl,
Spinning tales of a cosmic whirl.
Shooting stars with winks so sly,
Pizza sauce beneath the sky.

Galaxies flirt with comet's tail,
Cosmic giggles on a solar sail.
Asteroids munch on fruity treats,
While black holes hide in merry beats.

Laughter echoes through the void,
Cosmic cupcakes, never destroyed.
Planetary friends in jelly space,
All unite in this starlit race.

An Ode to the Gleaming Sphere

Oh, you sparkly orb, so grand!
Full of dreams and pizza stand.
With rings made from sweet fairy floss,
You twinkle like a boss, oh, gloss!

Your atmosphere, a cheerful brew,
Where clouds drink tea and cuddle too.
Cupcake comets race your face,
Joining in a cosmic chase.

The sun winks with a cheeky grin,
While Saturn giggles, spins, and spins.
Oh, gleaming sphere of pure delight,
You make our hearts feel oh so light!

Bouncing suns and flirty light,
In stardust dances we take flight.
Your dazzling glow, a joyful beam,
Fills the universe with a dream.

Reflections in Galactic Pools

In cosmic ponds, we splash and play,
With starry fish in ballet sway.
Jellybean planets swirl around,
In this sweet space, joy is found.

Reflections giggle as we dive,
In glittery waters, we feel alive.
Singing songs to the moonlit tide,
With giggling stars as our guide.

Space ducks quack a silly tune,
While comets join, a feathered swoon.
Splashing laughter fills the air,
Cosmic fun beyond compare.

In pools of joy, we swirl and glide,
Chasing dreams, oh, what a ride!
With cosmic friends, we sit and swoon,
Beneath the laughter of the moon.

The Spirit of Celestial Romance

In the cosmos where lovers meet,
Planets buzz with a fizzy beat.
Dancing stars in pairs of fun,
Twirl together 'til the day is done.

Romantic waves of stardust fly,
As Cupid's rocket zooms on high.
With each wink, a nova's birth,
Love erupts across the Earth.

Nebulae whisper in a flirty rhyme,
In this enchanted space, we climb.
Asteroids giggle with glee,
As they crash into destiny.

With sparkling joy and cosmic cheer,
Lovers' laughter we all hear.
A universe painted in delight,
In the spirit of love, so bright!

Woven Stardust Dreams

In the sky where giggles play,
Even stars have things to say.
They twinkle with a quirky flair,
And tumble through the cosmic air.

Comets zoom past with a wink,
Leaving trails like spilled ink.
Galaxies whirl with a silly dance,
A jest in the great expanse.

Clouds of candy fluffs appear,
Joking around, bringing cheer.
Black holes suck in laughter loud,
While planets twirl, feeling proud.

So laugh with the stars up above,
In the vastness, there's so much love.
Woven dreams of stardust bright,
Make the universe feel just right.

Enigmas of the Shining Sphere

Mystery wraps the glowing orb,
Tickling thoughts that we absorb.
"Why do moons wear goofy hats?"
And stars debate like chatty cats?

The sun plays hide and seek at dawn,
Shooting rays, scattering 'til they're gone.
Planets bicker, 'Who's the best?'
While comets zoom and take a rest.

Asteroids roll with a clumsy grace,
Jokes that can brighten up any space.
Nebulas chuckle in colors bright,
Radiating joy in the quiet night.

So ponder on this cosmic jest,
Laughter is truly what we need best.
In this sphere where enigmas dwell,
Let's dance with the stars and yell!

Love Letters in the Nebula

In clouds where lovebirds coyly dwell,
They send sweet notes, and giggles swell.
Stars scribble on bright cosmic sheets,
While planets blush, shy in their beats.

"Do you like my rings?" one does muse,
While chasing the hues of cosmic blues.
They flirt with comets, twirling so spry,
In a dance that lifts them high.

Letters sealed with stardust spark,
Whisper secrets in the dark.
Unraveled dreams across the sky,
Where love is light, and hopes can fly.

So send your heart on a gleaming flight,
Through galaxies sparkling in the night.
In this nebula of silly sighs,
Love's laughter echoes and never dies.

Tales of the Brilliant Sphere

Gather 'round for tales so bright,
Of twinkling wonders in the night.
Each tale's a giggle, a cosmic tease,
From starry shores and moonlit seas.

Planets prank with a spin and whirl,
Jupiter chuckles, Saturn gives a twirl.
The Milky Way's a winding path,
Where every turn can spark a laugh.

Shooting stars race to steal the show,
While black holes hum a soft, deep flow.
Galactic giggles bounce and soar,
Tales that tickle forevermore.

So listen close to the astral cheer,
Of brilliant spheres that dance so near.
In this cosmic playground, bright and grand,
The universe laughs, hand in hand.

Echoes of a Melodic Sphere

Bouncing balls of cosmic cheer,
Dancing comets, never fear!
Stars in hats, light up the night,
Wobbling asteroids take flight.

Puppies of the galaxy bark,
Jupiter's moons join the spark.
Playful planets spin around,
In this circus, joy is found.

Singing suns in silly tones,
Tickle Saturn's rings like bones.
Woozy meteors make a wish,
Cosmic giggles, what a dish!

So grab a slice of space-time pie,
With laughter, let our spirits fly!
In the universe's grand parade,
Silly echoes never fade.

Celestial Whispers

Whispers float through starry skies,
Talking moons with sleepy sighs.
A wink from Mars, a giggle here,
Shooting stars toast with cold beer!

Galactic friends with funny quirks,
Galaxies twirl, and nothing irks.
Nibbling on some nebula treats,
Cosmic patrol in silly fleets.

Wobbling worlds play hide and seek,
Each twinkling light has its own cheek.
Kittens of the cosmos chase,
Sassy comets, a funny race!

Space-time bends with laughter's reach,
Planets giggle, oh what a speech!
In the silence, joy does bloom,
Cheers from the starlit room!

Love in the Ether

Cupid's arrow flies through space,
Bumping into a comet's face.
Giggles shared on moons so bright,
Love in the ether, pure delight!

A serenade from a black hole,
Socks and sandals, that's the goal!
Asteroids fall for a sweet kiss,
In the cosmos, we find bliss.

Planetary hearts race and soar,
Cosmic crushes we can't ignore.
With laughter, stars begin to twirl,
In the galaxy, love's a whirl!

From solar flares to distant seas,
Parting clouds with playful ease.
Join the dance of stellar grace,
Love in the ether, a warm embrace!

Elegy of the Morning Star

Oh, morning star with cheeky grin,
How did you sneak under my skin?
Winking at the sleepy Earth,
Your bright giggles bring us mirth.

Chasing dreams on dawn's parade,
Who knew a star's glow could invade?
With coffee cups, we sip and chat,
About life, love, and silly hats!

Lost in the orbit of your charm,
No need for worry, you'll keep warm.
As night fades, we say goodbye,
With playful laughter, in the sky.

So rest a while, sweet morning light,
We'll meet again, oh, what a sight!
In the galaxy's endless jest,
With giggling stars, we are truly blessed.

Odyssey of the Golden Goddess

Amid swirling clouds, she lost her shoe,
Chasing little stars, oh what a view!
Venus calls forth, with a wink and a grin,
Who knew space travel could spark such a spin?

Baking cosmic cookies, they puffed like dough,
Aliens joined in, putting on quite a show!
They danced on asteroids, sang silly tunes,
While comets whizzed by, playing air maroons!

With retro sunglasses, and a bright pink hat,
She strutted through rings, look at that, look at that!
Gravitational pull got her stuck in a whirl,
But laughter erupted as she gave it a twirl!

In her golden chariot, she steered to the right,
Past shining moons, beneath starlit light.
Giggling as space bees buzzed her way,
A goddess of joy, what a whimsical day!

Starlit Reflections

In the mirror of starlight, shadows do dance,
Whispers of giggles, in a cosmic romance.
Glittering laughter echoes through space,
As the waves of humor take off with grace.

A comet remarks, with a flick of its tail,
Isn't it funny, this joking prevail?
Stars wink knowingly, sharing their cheer,
While planets join in, "Come over here!"

Reflections of silliness shimmer and sway,
In the vast universe, where jokes come to play.
With moonbeams as music, they all spin around,
Creating a symphony, moonlight unbound!

And as the sun rises, they hold back a grin,
For laughter is timeless, where all fun begins.
Through cosmic delights, they bask in the thrill,
Sharing starlit reflections, a memory to fill.

Songs from the Veil of Venus

Beneath the bright veil, where laughter does unfurl,
A serenade's melody dances in twirl.
Silly notes flutter like petals in flight,
As melodies tickle the air through the night.

With harmonies twinkling, the planets all sway,
As Venus belts tunes in her own funny way.
Eclipsing their woes, they chuckle and bloat,
As stardust confetti flows out of her throat!

"Why did the black hole bring a ladder?" she sang,
"Because it heard the universe had such a slang!"
Guffaws from the moons made them dance with delight,
To the madcap content from Venus's height!

So in the vast cosmos, they sing loud and free,
Songs from a goddess, the whole galaxy.
Wrapped in the veil, joyous hearts all align,
Laughter and music, a sweet intertwine!

Aurora's Embrace

In the glow of the morn, a giggle takes flight,
Auroras are painting the sky bright and light.
With colors so silly, they slide and they chase,
Winking at Earth with a jovial grace.

"Catch me if you can!" the auroras shout bold,
As they frolic and shimmer in pinks, greens, and gold.
Froggy-shaped clouds leap, adding to the fun,
While sunbeams join in, they shimmer and run!

Each twisty delight brings bursts of pure cheer,
Planetary chuckles resound loud and clear.
Jokes from the cosmos echo through space,
Witty and clever, each line finds its place!

And as night creeps in, with twinkling surprise,
The auroras will wink with their vibrant disguise.
Entwined in a giggle, the heavens embrace,
For laughter's a cosmic and boundless grace!

Heartbeats of the Milky Way

In a galaxy far, stars play a game,
Shooting each other with names that blame.
My heart tries to dance, it's so out of tune,
As comets wink at me, like a cosmic cartoon.

Black holes sucking laughter, who will survive?
Jokes float through space, like bubbles they thrive.
Asteroids chuckle, they're quite the parade,
While aliens giggle at plans they've made.

Planets all spinning, but I've lost my place,
Got caught in a whirl of a cosmic embrace.
They say in the stars, romance fills the void,
But it's a mess here, oh boy, I'm destroyed!

Yet even in chaos, there's joy to be found,
In the rhythm of starlight, I twirl all around.
With each little heartbeat, the cosmos will sway,
Laughing together, in our Milky Way.

Chasing Cosmic Currents

Riding the waves of the solar wind,
I feel quite the thrill, where do I begin?
Stars wink in delight, as I float on by,
Chasing those currents, oh my, oh my!

A comet surfboard, I'm hanging ten,
Jupiter's storms can't stop my zen.
Astrophysical gags are the best kind of spritz,
As meteor showers rain down in bits.

Galactic taxi, are we nearly there?
Say, do you mind if I take a chair?
Warped by gravity, I'm stuck in a loop,
With space-dogs barking, oh what a group!

Yet laughter rings out through the starlit sea,
Chasing these currents is the best way to be.
With jokes in the ether, I'm flying afar,
In the hilarious dance of this cosmic bazaar.

A Radiant Soliloquy

In the calm of the night, let's hear my plea,
You, radiant moon, are you laughing at me?
I trip on stardust while trying to sway,
A lopsided tango in the Milky Way.

Rays of sunshine are teasing my hair,
While I fumble with words that float in the air.
Shooting stars scold me for my silly mistakes,
As I write love notes to my interstellar lakes.

Gravity played me, it pulled and it twisted,
My hopes for romance are a bit too brisked.
Yet through the supernova, I giggle and sigh,
Spinning in circles, all I can do is fly.

If laughter's the light that shines through the dark,
I'll wear it like glitter, like an astral spark.
In the dance of the cosmos, an outlandish play,
I'll sing my soliloquy in the Milky Way.

Harmonies of the Universe

Under the glow of a nearby star,
The universe hums; how bizarre, how bizarre!
With rhythm of comets, and bass from the sun,
I strum on my heartstrings, just having some fun.

Planets in line, making quite the show,
Each spin is a joke, or so I know.
Mars cracks a punchline, while Earth takes a bow,
As Saturn rolls laughter, saying, "Time's here now!"

Orchestras play with asteroids clapping,
Neptune's a tenor, while Pluto's still napping.
A symphony swirls in the galaxies bright,
As stars shine their giggles through the velvety night.

So come join the choir of all things absurd,
Where humor and music are happily stirred.
In the grand cosmic dance, we find our own groove,
Swaying together, in a rhythm that moves.

Siren Songs from Afar

In a galaxy not so wide,
There's a fish with a wink and a glide.
She sings to the stars with great cheer,
While aliens dance and shout, 'Oh dear!'

Her voice bounces off every moon,
Making them giggle, a silly tune.
Asteroids jiggle, comets spin,
A cosmic party, let the fun begin!

Little green folks bring chips and dip,
As they groove and they sway, oh what a trip!
They float like balloons, all light and spry,
With laughter echoing through the night sky.

So next time you gaze at the bright stars above,
Remember that space is a place filled with love.
Where fishy sirens and aliens prance,
Creating a universe of cosmic romance.

Luminous Echoes of Affection

In the glow of the moon's playful rays,
Lies a creature who loves to amaze.
With a wink and a twirl, it beams a light,
Making craters laugh through the cold, crisp night.

It juggles moon rocks like marbles, oh my!
While stardust tickles the clouds up high.
Nearby, a comet stops for a bite,
Sharing snacks with a joyful delight.

Laughter echoes through the cosmic foam,
As creatures wonder if this is home.
Love letters written in beams of green,
In the laughter of starlight, a silly scene.

The universe fills with giggles and cheer,
As stars hold hands, no room for fear.
In this whimsical dance, joy does thrive,
Under the glow, we feel so alive!

Stardust Serenade

In a spaceship shaped like a giant pie,
A chef with a mustache reaches for the sky.
He serves up stardust, crunch with a fizz,
"For a cosmic feast, this is how it is!"

With laughter and food flying everywhere,
The crew of odd ducks floats in the air.
A cat on a bassoon plays jazzy notes,
While robots tap dance in silver coats.

"Try the nebula salad, it's out of this world!"
A green alien twirls, his antennas unfurled.
As everyone munches on moons made of cheese,
The universe giggles, it's all just a tease!

So when you feel down, remember this crew,
Where laughter and stardust are always in view.
In a ship made of pie, with friends by your side,
You'll find that in space, joy never hides!

The Sublime Orb

On a planet that wiggles and giggles with glee,
Lives a sublime orb, so carefree.
It bounces and rolls, with humor galore,
Creating new games that we all can explore.

With a chuckle, it spins, sending ripples of joy,
While moonbeams jump in, just like a toy.
"Let's play tag!" it cheers, "I'll always win!"
The stars roll their eyes, 'Here we go again!'

They race across rings, through light years they soar,
As laughter weaves in every galactic door.
The sublime orb glows with a wink and a nod,
Collecting giggles, like gifts from the odd.

So if you feel heavy, like gravity's glue,
Look up to the sky, find the orb—yes, it's true!
In its merry dance, adventures await,
A universe spinning with humor and fate!

Celestial Dreams Unfurled

In the sky where laughter dwells,
Stars play tricks, casting spells.
Planets dance with silly grace,
Comets giggle, floating in space.

Meteor showers rain down jokes,
While Saturn's rings toast with folks.
The moon, a jester, winks at night,
Spreading joy with its silver light.

Galaxies swirl in goofy spins,
Twirling tales of cosmic wins.
Asteroids roll with a clumsy cheer,
Singing songs from yesteryear.

So let's toast to the cosmic jest,
Where laughter echoes, never rests.
In this vast venue of delight,
Every star shines bright, all right!

Horizons of Desire

On the edge where dreams collide,
Planets chase with whimsy wide.
In cosmic shops, love sells for free,
Let's bargain with stars for glee!

Flirting moons with rosy cheeks,
Whisper sweet nothings, no critiques.
Mars blushes red, challenges the sun,
In a comedy of hearts, we have fun.

Asteroids toss around clues,
Telling tales of galactic blues.
The universe twirls, a playful tease,
In this dance, we find our ease.

So let's mingle in this celestial spree,
Where giggles echo, wild and free.
Horizons stretch with a wink so sly,
In the cosmos, love will never die!

The Language of Light

Flashes of doodles paint the sky,
Light beams chatter, oh my, oh my!
Nebulas scribble in vibrant hues,
Sending messages, amusing clues.

Photon whispers tickle the ear,
Twinkling stars spreading good cheer.
Sunbeams snicker at moonlit pale,
Crafting tales with a carnival trail.

Lightyears stretch in jolly jest,
Tickling time, it's truly the best.
Galaxies giggle in radiant streams,
Filling the cosmos with silly dreams.

With every beam, laughter ignites,
The universe dances, oh what a sight!
In the language of light, we find,
A harmony that's truly one of a kind!

Echoes Beneath the Radiant Veil

Beneath the veil where secrets play,
Echoes of laughter dance all day.
Winking stars share their latest tease,
Cosmic whispers carried by the breeze.

Hidden worlds spark jokes divine,
As birds of space sip on starlit wine.
Riding comets with goofy flair,
In this realm, joys freely share.

Galactic giggles bounce around,
In this treasure trove, fun is found.
Each twinkle tells a story bright,
Of silly antics in the night.

So let's celebrate this merry quest,
In cosmic joy, we are blessed.
Under radiant veils, we dream and play,
In the echoes of laughter, we find our way!

The Glow of Infinite Longing

Beneath the starry skies we chat,
With love notes written on a cat.
Each wink, a spark, a teasing jest,
What if we both just need a rest?

In cosmic cafes, we sip on dreams,
With stardust sprinkles in our creams.
You order love, I ask for flair,
As planets laugh, I twirl my hair.

When comets race and rockets zoom,
You steal my fries; it's quite the doom.
In galactic fun, our hearts collide,
While solar winds become our guide.

So here we are, with moonlit grace,
Navigating through this silly space.
With giggles bright and laughter grand,
Let's venture off, just hand in hand.

Astral Love Letters

In the mailbox of the Milky Way,
I found your notes, signed 'Love from Play.'
Each letter floated, a feathered quill,
With goofy hearts and ample thrill.

You wrote of stars that danced and twirled,
Of intergalactic flags unfurled.
But did you mean 'a date' for brunch?
Or just a cosmic, chocolate munch?

Your doodles made the skies so bright,
A spaceman twirling in the night.
With Martian jokes about our fate,
You make it hard to contemplate!

We'll pen a book of our own weird tales,
With lovebirds soaring on comet trails.
In this vast universe, laughter reigns,
As we scribble joy on starry plains.

Hidden Gardens of the Sky

In the clouds, we found a sprout,
With giggles floating all about.
A garden of quirky comets grew,
With flowers blooming in a hue!

The daisies danced with neon rays,
As we painted planets in funny ways.
Bumblebees wore capes for fun,
While stars planned parties, one by one.

Each petal whispered cosmic dreams,
Of candy rivers and moonbeam teams.
We tossed our wishes to the breeze,
As laughter sprouted from the trees.

Through hidden paths of sparkling light,
We pranced until the edge of night.
So come along, let's skip and twirl,
In gardens where our giggles swirl.

A Canvas of Cosmic Light

With a brush made of stardust, I paint the skies,
A swirl of laughter where the moon flies.
Each streak a smile, each star a cheer,
As I splash the cosmos with joy, oh dear!

The sun winks brightly, it's quite the sight,
As I doodle rockets that fly in flight.
My canvas giggles, it beckons a call,
To join this art where we can all sprawl.

With suns that cartwheel and planets that sing,
We frolic in hues of a magical spring.
Each brushstroke dances, a whimsical play,
A masterpiece where dreams find their sway.

So grab your palette, my playful friend,
Let's color the cosmos, on laughter depend.
In this gallery of joy, we'll surely delight,
With a canvas alive, shining ever so bright.

Embracing the Celestial Tide

In the sky, a disco ball,
Planets twirl, as if at a ball.
Dancing moons with socks so bright,
Giggles echo through the night.

Stars wear hats, and comets wink,
Who knew space could make you think?
Jupiter's belly is round and wide,
He shakes it off with cosmic pride.

A sunbeam tickles a starry nose,
While Martians host a fashion show.
Asteroids rolling by with flair,
Gracing the scene with wild hair.

Saturn spins, all rings askew,
'I'm late to brunch!' shouts the blue.
In this cosmic giggle spree,
Joy is boundless, wild, and free.

Visions of Celestial Elysium

In a dream where stardust flows,
Aliens trade the wildest clothes.
Zany creatures of a laugh,
Play hopscotch on a stellar path.

Meteors zoom past in haste,
'Excuse me!'—not one, but three, a race.
Galactic jokes fly like light,
Making black holes laugh with delight.

Uranus blushes, losing its cool,
'They can't see my rings, what a fool!'
Cosmic giggles fill the void,
Where silly dreams cannot be destroyed.

Nebulas dance in rainbow hues,
Painting the sky with laughter's muse.
In this realm where all is fun,
Stars poke fun at everyone.

Celestial Fusion

Two stars meet for a cosmic date,
One brings snacks, the other, fate.
They build a joke that shimmers bright,
And sing a song that lasts all night.

Black holes laugh at their own depth,
'You can't escape, but we're not inept!'
Galaxies swirl with a twisty cheer,
As light years pass, they hold things dear.

Quasars scream with radiant beams,
Filling the dark with giggliest dreams.
In this mix, the laughs align,
In cosmic chaos, joy does shine.

Comets join, a raucous crowd,
Shooting stars, hey, aren't we loud?
In the vastness where we all reside,
Let laughter be our galactic guide.

Reflections in the Cosmos

Mirrors crack in a supernova blare,
Showing planets with funny hair.
Pulsars blink with witty flair,
As they frolic in cosmic air.

Stars sit down for a tea-filled jest,
'Who's the brightest? I'm the best!'
In their games, they find the light,
Conjuring chuckles through the night.

A neutron star sips cosmic waves,
While time bends and giggles misbehave.
The Milky Way, a dance floor grand,
Hosts a party that's truly unplanned.

Reflecting joy in every hue,
From realms unknown, they giggle anew.
In the universe's endless play,
Laughter reigns, come what may.

Celestial Serenade

Stars in pajamas, just chilling at night,
Dancing on rooftops, oh what a sight!
The moon wore a hat, quite big and round,
While comets played tag, without making a sound.

Space cats in rocket ships zooming by fast,
Nibbling on stardust, what a real blast!
Galaxies giggling in cosmic delight,
Bouncing off asteroids, oh what a flight!

Planets are singing, a jolly old song,
Jupiter's rhymes keep us smiling along.
Saturn brought cookies, each ring holds a treat,
While Mars serves up lemonade, chilly and sweet.

In the vast universe, laughter takes wing,
Aliens harmonize, such joy they bring!
Cosmos is laughing, it's perfectly clear,
Together in stardust, we cheer and we cheer!

Glistening in the Twilight

Dew on the grass sparkles like dreams,
Fireflies twirling in whimsical themes.
Crickets are crooning with comic delight,
A concert of chirps, it's a funny sight.

Trees giggle softly, whispering gossip,
Squirrels in wigs take a rumor-filled trip.
Moonbeams tickle the clouds way up high,
While stars tease the night with a cheeky sigh.

Puddles reflect the chaos below,
As frogs in tuxedos put on quite a show.
Toads are the judges, they croak and they croon,
Awarding the prize to the best-dressed raccoon.

Laughter and starlight mix in the air,
Joyful absurdity everywhere!
As night takes a bow, let the silly persist,
Finding fun in the twinkle, we simply can't miss!

Whispers of the Evening Star

Evening Star winks, a mischievous glow,
Chatting with fireflies, putting on a show.
Breezes are giggling, tickling the trees,
While shadows play tag, teasing with ease.

Nights are more fun with a chuckle or two,
As owls share jokes that are old and quite true.
The groundhogs laugh softly, sharing a grin,
Creating their own little whirlwind of whim.

The moon strums a tune on a silver-lined harp,
As night critters gather, singing out sharp.
Shooting stars swoosh, leaving trails of delight,
Winking at mortals all lost in the night.

Whispers of joy echo softly around,
In the magical twilight where laughter is found.
Nature holds secrets, so silly, so bright,
Together we giggle beneath the starlight!

Ethereal Echoes

Clouds with faces drift lazily by,
Mimicking dancers under the sky.
Rain falls like confetti, a bubbly surprise,
Making puddles giggle, bringing joy to our eyes.

Balloons made of starlight float high in the air,
With wishes and dreams tangled in hair.
A flock of exuberant birds sings in tune,
While butterflies laugh, fluttering soon.

Comets wear glasses, looking absurd,
Racing through cosmos, oh how they've stirred!
Galactic assembly of chuckles and charms,
As planets unite with their whimsical arms.

In the echoes of laughter, the universe spins,
Crafting joy from the chaos, where humor begins.
A tapestry woven with giggles and cheer,
In the glorious cosmos, let's all persevere!

Celestial Longing

In a galaxy far, far away,
A planet winks, come what may.
Love's gravity pulls, it's quite absurd,
Like trying to find a lost bird.

With aliens bobbing in bright costumes,
Flirting with rocks and space mushrooms.
A comet zips by, oh what a sight,
As I dodge space debris in flight.

Heartbeats echo through the void,
In my rocket, I feel quite buoyed.
But did I just send a love tweet?
Or was that just a snack to eat?

So here's to love in unknown skies,
With starry eyes and silly sighs.
We'll dance on rings, what a delight,
In this cosmic love, day turns to night.

Starlit Revelations

Beneath a sky that glows and swirls,
I ponder love, as comet curls.
Is romance just a space-time joke?
Like seeking truth in a puff of smoke?

Meteor showers shower down,
Falling stars make me wear a frown.
Did I just wish for pizza pie?
Oh, that's not love, let's not lie!

A UFO zips by with a grin,
Could they be the ones, or just a tin?
I toss a heart like it's a moon,
But they zoom off, how rude, soon!

With every blip upon my screen,
I laugh at what love might have been.
In the vastness, I still hold tight,
To funny dreams of cosmic flight.

The Art of Cosmic Romance

Floating through space with flowers in hand,
Hoping a probe might understand.
Martians tease with a cheeky grin,
What might love with them begin?

My heart beats like a pulsar bright,
For cosmic flings and wild delight.
I wrote a poem to the moon,
But it just hummed a silly tune.

Rockets zoom, and lasers flash,
A love story moves oh so rash.
Can I charm a star with my song?
Or would it just take me along?

When cuddles turn to asteroid fights,
And moonlit dances end in bites.
The galaxy laughs, it's all in fun,
For every heart, there's someone, everyone!

Songs of an Interstellar Heart

In the cosmic dance, I twirl and spin,
With alien voices, we laugh and grin.
Who knew love thrived on distant stars?
Beyond the reach of earthly bars?

Singing with nebulae, bright and bold,
Love stories woven, unruly and old.
A black hole pulls, but I refuse,
To let it dampen my spacey muse!

Spaceship karaoke, what a show,
But who's the judge? I'd like to know.
With every note, a comet flies,
Sing sweetly, under glowing skies!

Though planets may clash and stars may fade,
Our cosmic hearts will never be weighed.
So here's a tune from me to you,
Love's the ultimate space debut!

Celestial Garden

In a garden where stars like veggies grow,
Martians trim roses with a disco show.
Planets roll by on their cosmic wheels,
Singing to the moon about their meals.

Saturn's rings bake pies in the sky,
While Jupiter giggles and passes by.
Uranus is laughing, quite the silly lad,
With a twinkling sense that's utterly mad.

Cherries from Orbits, ripe and round,
Made by the comets that dance on the ground.
Galactic fruits juggling in flight,
Whispering secrets beneath starlit light.

Dandelions in nebulae spread their seeds,
Tickling the stardust where laughter leads.
Every bloom tells a cosmic joke,
In this garden where starlight spoke.

Petals of the Morning Star

Petals pop up with a humorous flair,
Giggles erupting from everywhere.
Morning's got puns sprouting like grass,
Each one so silly, you'd snort and pass!

A sunbeam dances, doing a jig,
Tickling petals, making them gig.
Dewdrops drip like laughter from leaves,
Echoing joy, as each blossom achieves.

Silly star sprinkles dance on the breeze,
Making daisies wobble and tease.
"Why did the tulip cross the road?" they say,
"To blossom and bloom in a funny way!"

Colors collide with a playful scheme,
As birds sing with a giggly beam.
The morning star winks with glee,
Setting the petals as merry as can be!

Enchanted Skies

In the enchanted skies, where clouds tickle stars,
Galaxies twirl like whimsical cars.
The moon plays cards with mischievous sprites,
While comets burst forth in giggling flights.

Starfish in space throw a cosmic ball,
Joking with meteors, having a ball.
"Do you know how to tell if stars are late?"
"Check their time zone and giggle at fate!"

The sun wears shades, acting quite cool,
While the earth sends up a giggly drool.
Rain showers toss little giggles like seeds,
Making the whole universe chuckle with needs.

Planets do cartwheels, spinning with joy,
As asteroids mingle; what a fun ploy!
In these enchanted skies of laughter and light,
The universe winks at the joy of the night.

Harmony of the Cosmic Rose

In a garden of roses, cosmic and bright,
Blooming with laughter in the glowing night.
Each petal is quirky, tells a jest or two,
Even the thorns have a giggle or hue.

"Why do roses love the cosmic dance?"
"Because they can twirl and not miss a chance!"
Their fragrance floats up, a playful delight,
As stars clap their hands in joyous flight.

A cosmic rose turns to face the sun,
Whispering secrets, ready for fun.
"Keep blooming, dear friend, don't wilt or fade,
Life's too short for an unfun parade!"

So twirl like the petals, embrace the lush cheer,
Join the cosmic laughter, let go of the fear.
For in the harmony of roses that play,
Lies the giggle of life, lighting our way.

Lost in a Galaxy of Dreams

In a galaxy bright, where wishes take flight,
I tripped on a star, what a comical sight!
I danced with the comets, they laughed with glee,
Until I got tangled in space-time debris.

With aliens chuckling at my clumsy show,
I tried to impress them with moonwalking flow.
But fell on a planet made solely of cheese,
Now I'm stuck in a sandwich, oh help, if you please!

Floating on clouds shaped like giant tarantulas,
I asked for directions, they whispered in cantulas.
I followed a trail of sweet stardust and cream,
But woke on a couch—it was all just a dream!

So here's to the cosmos, where humor is grand,
I'll keep my space helmet, my trusty command.
For the laughs are the map to this cosmic delight,
I'll skip with the stars till the dawn's early light.

The Symphony of the Night Sky

A trumpet from Mars, oh what a surprise,
The moon's got rhythm, under swirling skies.
Stars strum their strings, and planets collide,
In the orchestra of night, there's nowhere to hide!

Comets on flutes play catchy old tunes,
While asteroids thump like big, bouncy balloons.
The milky way dances, a twirling ballet,
Dressed up in stardust, it's quite the display!

Meteor showers punctuate with a bang,
"Is that a shooting star?!" the giggling kids sang.
But all the while, I sat in my chair,
With popcorn and soda, without a care.

The symphony pulsed, oh what a delight!
Though the performance could last all night.
The laughter of planets, the joy of the sun,
Every note played reminds us, we're all just here for fun!

Stellar Embraces

In the arms of the cosmos, I found a big hug,
From a star that was winking, so warm and snug.
I twirled with the galaxies, spinning with flair,
But bumped into Neptune—apologies there!

"Oh dear, you're quite cold!" I giggled and said,
As he shivered my way, his blue aura spread.
"Let's warm up, dear friend, with a blanket of light,
And bake us some cookies, they'll be out of sight!"

We danced under starlight, a humorous scene,
With Saturn's rings clapping, it felt like a dream.
Asteroids cheered, throwing confetti above,
In a stellar embrace, how could we not love?

So here's to the laughter, the joy that it brings,
To moonlit adventures and whimsical things.
With each cosmic hug, let's add to our cheer,
In the universe's arms, we've nothing to fear!

The Poetry of Sparkling Dreams

In a garden of stars, I tried to compose,
A poem of laughter, with glittery prose.
The sun peeked and giggled, "What's this all about?"
"I thought poets were wise, not fumbling about!"

I wrote on the winds with a twinkling quill,
But the comets kept swooping, giving me a chill.
"Enough with your rhymes!" cried the moon in a jest,
"You'll write us a sonnet, or we'll never let rest!"

With sparkles like flowers, I scribbled at night,
A sonnet on stardust, oh, what a delight!
Each line danced and shimmered, a cheerful refrain,
As the clouds puffed around, they giggled in vain.

So here's to the dreams, both silly and bright,
To the laughter we share in the soft silver light.
For in cosmic poetry, we find our true seam,
In the sparkling embrace of a whimsical dream.

www.ingramcontent.com/pod-product-compliance
Lightning Source LLC
Chambersburg PA
CBHW051641160426
43209CB00004B/743